THE STORY BEHIND THE SYMBOL

U.S. FLAG

PowerKiDS press

Gail Parman

Published in 2027 by The Rosen Publishing Group, Inc.
2544 Clinton Street, Buffalo, NY 14224

Portions of this work were originally authored by Cecelia H. Brannon and published as *Zoom in on American Symbols: Zoom in on the US Flag*. All new material in this edition is authored by Gail Parman.

Editor: Tricia Hoffman
Book Design: Beeline Media and Design

Photo Credits: Cover, p. 1 jonathandav/Shutterstock.com; p. cover, 1, 5, 7, 9, 11, 13, 15, 17, 19, 21 Realstockvector/Shutterstock.com; p. 4 Bridgeman Art Library/Bridgeman Art Library; p. 5 Your Hand Please/Shutterstock.com; p. 6 Bill Chizek/Shutterstock.com; p. 7 ChicagoPhotographer/Shutterstock.com; p. 8, 10, 12, 14, 16 Public Domain/Shutterstock.com; p. 9 Everett Collection/Shutterstock.com; p. 11 Nixx Photography/Shutterstock.com; p. 13 Dorti/Shutterstock.com; p. 15 Library of Congress/Library of Congress; p. 17 Smithsonian/Smithsonian; p. 18, 19 Dennis MacDonald/Shutterstock.com; p. 20 Wikipedia/Wikipedia; p. 21 Rawpixel.com/Shutterstock.com

Cataloging-in-Publication Data
Names: Parman, Gail.
Title: U.S. Flag / Gail Parman.
Description: Buffalo, New York : PowerKids Press, 2027. | Series: The story behind the symbol | Includes glossary and index.
Identifiers: ISBN 9781499458190 (pbk.) | ISBN 9781499458206 (library bound) | ISBN 9781499458213 (ebook)
Subjects: LCSH: Flags--United States--Juvenile literature. | Emblems, National--United States--Juvenile literature
Classification: LCC CR113.P377 2027 | DDC 929.920973--dc23

Printed in China

CPSIA Compliance Information: Batch #QSPK27. For Further Information contact Rosen Publishing at 1-800-237-9932.

CONTENTS

The History of the American Flag

The red, white, and blue of the American flag is instantly recognizable. Today, the flag includes 50 white stars set on a blue rectangle. Those stars represent the 50 states. The flag also has 13 red stripes and 13 white stripes. These stripes represent the 13 original colonies that formed the country 250 years ago. But how did this flag come to be?

In the mid-1770s, the American colonies were fighting to be free from Great Britain. The **colonists** needed a **symbol** of the new nation they were trying to form. They wanted something to look up to and to show that they were separate from the British. They needed a flag.

The Revolutionary War was fought between the American colonies and Great Britain. In 1778, France joined on the side of the colonists. After that, many other countries joined to fight against Britain too.

Search for the Flag

George Washington, the general of the Continental Army, began the search for an official flag in 1775. While trying to free Boston from British rule, he raised a flag known as the Grand Union flag. This flag had red and white stripes with a union jack (the British flag) in the corner. It was not the first official flag of the United States, but it was the first time colonists had declared themselves separate from the British.

Another famous flag was the "Don't Tread on Me" flag, which was designed in 1775. The flag showed a snake atop the words "Don't Tread on Me." This flag was a **protest** against the British treatment of the colonists. It inspired the American colonists to stick up for themselves.

Though not official, the Grand Union flag is often considered the first American flag. In 1777, the union jack was removed and replaced with stars.

The Official Flag

The United States' first flag was most likely designed by Francis Hopkinson, a New Jersey congressman and signer of the Declaration of Independence. Many people believe that Betsy Ross, a **seamstress** and **upholsterer**, sewed the first American flag. Ross passed that story along to her children and grandchildren, but no one has been able to prove that she made the first flag.

Francis Hopkinson

The first flag had 13 stripes of red and white, and 13 stars on a blue background. Each star and stripe represented the 13 colonies that would become a new nation. In the early years, flag makers decided how to arrange the stars. Sometimes, they were in rows. Other times, they formed a circle.

Betsy Ross is said to have sewn the first American flag. In the early years, there was no rule for where the stars on the flag should go.

A Symbol of Hope

The Revolutionary War began in 1775. It lasted for eight years. As the war went on, the flag became a symbol of hope for many Americans. In 1777, the Continental Congress decided the flag would be "thirteen stripes, alternate red and white; that the union be thirteen stars, white in a blue field, representing a new **Constellation.**"

Each of the flag's colors has meaning. These colors were not chosen by accident. Red symbolizes hardiness and **valor.** It honors the sacrifices of the people who fought for the country's independence. White represents purity and innocence and the hope for peace and unity. And blue stands for vigilance, **perseverance**, and justice, especially the country's commitment to fairness and equality.

Flag Day is celebrated each year on June 14. It is a day that honors the date in 1777 when the official design was chosen.

The 13 Original Colonies

When the first flag was made, there were 13 colonies. They were Delaware, Pennsylvania, New Jersey, Georgia, Connecticut, Massachusetts, Maryland, South Carolina, New Hampshire, Virginia, New York, North Carolina, and Rhode Island.

After the Revolution, the United States became its own nation. The country soon began to grow. By 1795, two more states, Vermont and Kentucky, had been added. Two more stars were added to the flag. It was decided the original 13 stripes would remain, as a reminder of the nation's beginnings.

The flag in 1795.

There have been 27 versions of the American flag. Today's flag is the first version that has lasted longer than 50 years.

More States, More Stars

The flag in 1861.

The United States continued to grow. More states joined the nation, so more and more stars had to be added. By 1861, there were 34 stars on the flag. But this was another difficult time for the nation. The Civil War had begun, and 11 states **seceded** from the Union, wishing to create their own country. President Abraham Lincoln refused to let the nation split. He even refused to remove stars from the flag, despite the fact that the Southern states were calling themselves the Confederate States of America and had their own flag.

The flag continued to change as the nation did. After the Civil War, a 36-star flag had to be created for the additions of West Virginia and Nevada. The nation continued growing for another hundred years.

Abraham Lincoln was president during the Civil War years. He was killed just days after it officially ended.

Flying Proudly

Today, "Old Glory" is a common nickname for the U.S. flag. The original "Old Glory" flag was flown by William Driver, a sea captain from Massachusetts who lived in the South during the Civil War. The flag was made in 1824 by Driver's mother and given to him as a birthday present. Even though he lived in the South, he refused to fly the Confederate flag and instead flew Old Glory proudly over his home. Many times throughout the war, Confederates tried to destroy the flag. But it survived, and "Old Glory" saw the nation whole again.

Grave marker of William Driver

Today, Driver's "Old Glory" can be seen at the National Museum of American History in Washington, D.C.

The American Flag Today

The version of the American flag as we know it today has been in use for more than 60 years. It was officially adopted on July 4, 1960, when Hawaii became the last state to join the United States of America. There is a proposed flag with 51 stars, in case another state is added.

The American flag is an important symbol that must be treated with respect. In 1942, President Franklin D. Roosevelt approved the guidelines for the treatment of the flag. For example, the flag may be displayed from sunrise until sunset every day, unless it is raining or snowing. It must be raised quickly, and lowered with care. When displayed flat or hung on a wall, the stars must be to the left as a person is looking at it.

There are a few places where the flag must fly day and night, even during bad weather. Some of them are the White House in Washington, D.C., Fort McHenry in Baltimore, Maryland, and the U.S. Marine Corps Memorial in Arlington, Virginia.

Around the World

The American flag can be seen outside of the United States. Not only is it flown at every U.S. **embassy** in every country across the world, but it has also been planted in many other places.

Robert Peary

In 1909, explorer Robert Peary planted the American flag his wife had sewn at the North Pole. In 1945, U.S. Marines raised a flag in Iwo Jima, showing they had beaten the Japanese army and ended World War II. In 1963, mountaineer Barry Bishop placed the American flag on Mount Everest, which is the highest point on Earth.

The American flag has influenced the design of many other country's flags, such as Liberia, Chile, Malaysia, and Uruguay.

Probably the most famous planting of the flag occurred in 1969, when the crew of Apollo 11 placed the American flag on the moon.

Activity: Learn to Fold a Flag

Knowing how to correctly fold a flag into a neat triangle shows honor and respect. Find a friend and practice these steps.

1. Hold the flag waist-high so that its surface is parallel to the ground. Then, fold the flag in half lengthwise, placing the lower half of the flag (the stripes) over the blue and white field of stars.

2. Fold the flag lengthwise again, so that the blue field is on the outside.

3. Make a triangular fold by bringing the corner of the striped corner up to meet the top of the flag (the open part).

4. Turn the point inward parallel to the open edge. Then, continue folding in this manner. When the flag is completely folded, the field of blue will be the only thing visible.

Glossary

colonist A person who lives in a new country.

constellation A group of stars that make a pattern or image.

embassy A place where people represent their own country in a foreign country.

perseverance Working hard to do something, despite facing difficulty.

protest A statement or action that shows disapproval.

seamstress A woman whose job is sewing.

secede To stop being a member.

symbol A thing that stands in or represents something else.

upholsterer Someone who makes fabric covering for furniture.

valor Great courage in the face of danger, especially in battle.

Index

Learn More

American Flag

https://easyscienceforkids.com/flag-of-usa/

Learn more about America's flag, as well as other flags from around the world.

Flag of the United States of America

https://kids.britannica.com/kids/article/Flag-of-the-United-States-of-America/624849

This Britannica Kids article discusses the national flag of the United States and the history behind it.

Publisher's note to educators and parents: Our editors have carefully reviewed these websites to ensure that they are suitable for students. Many websites change frequently, however, and we cannot guarantee that a site's future contents will continue to meet our high standards of quality and educational value. Be advised that students should be closely supervised whenever they access the Internet.